Restless Nights

BROOKE ROSEN

ILLUSTRATED BY
DANIELA SHTURMAN

Copyright © 2023 Brooke Rosen.

All rights reserved. This book is protected by copyright. No part of this book may be reproduced or transmitted in any form or by any means, including as photocopies or scanned-in or other electronic copies, or utilized by any information storage and retrieval system without written permission from the copyright owner.

Distribution and design by Bublish

ISBN: 978-1-647047-81-8 (paperback)
ISBN: 978-1-647047-79-5 (eBook)

Printed in the United States of America.

Dear Reader, when I was four years old, I wrote my first book, and since then, I've never been able to resist a pencil and a blank piece of paper. As I grew older, my writing shifted from fiction to personal stories about the challenges life threw at me, but insecurities stopped me from sharing my work. However, as I meet more and more young people who have faced similar challenges, I've come to deeply appreciate the strong support system of professionals, family and friends that surrounds me. I believe no one deserves to go through life feeling alone, which is why I have chosen not to let fear hold me back from telling my story. Writing is the glue that holds me together, and I want my words to do the same for others. I want to give voice to those too scared to speak and teach empathy to those who don't understand. When you read my words, I hope you uncover the stories of millions.

1

You break my heart
but fuel my words.

Cry Me A River

Cry me a river.
Let the rain come splashing down.
Let the seas rise.
Let me float away.
Cry me a river to my peace of mind.
And if they miss me, let them know I tried.
And if they, too, cry a river ever so strong,
let them know I understand.
Let them know I will wait for them,
here on the other side.

Red Wine

He stained her skin.
Although she wishes to move on,
every time she looks down, she sees a piece of him.
She wanted the rush.
She longed for adventure.
But just like red wine and a white dress,
the two were destined for tragedy instead of success.

Teardrops

It's quiet in my dark, cold room.
Surrounding me is memorabilia from my childhood.
Each piece tells its own story.
Still, my heart feels empty.
My bed is warm, but the tears that flow down my face are warmer.
Please don't feel bad for me.
That is not my intention.
If only you could understand, I'm happiest when my vision begins to blur
as teardrops race each other to the bottom of my chin.

Camera Roll

I keep the pictures we took.
I don't know why.
When I come across them, I quickly scroll away.
Those images are the last things I want to see.
But it's comforting to know at least they're mine.

Cracks In The Wall

Most of our fights were left unresolved.
Each time a reminder, we should put out the flame.
But we never did.
Instead, we took our pain and buried it out back.
Hidden from the world.
Hidden from us.
And when we ran out of space, we stored it in our walls.
Until our house became weaker than our hearts.
All because we were too young to let go.
Too scared to move on.

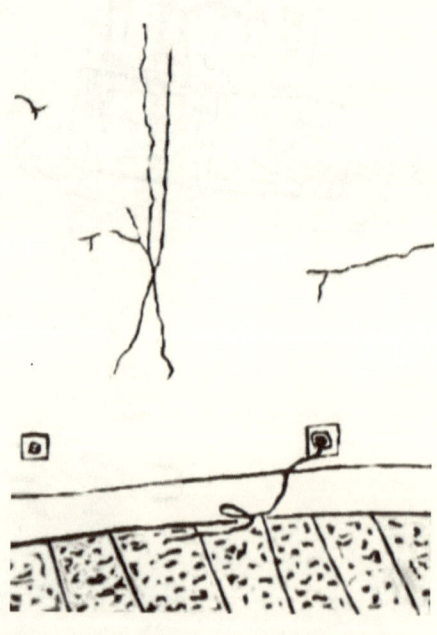

Nowhere To Go

Beneath the surface of my skin lies a soul,
and it cries.
How badly it wants to escape.
How it aches to rest.
But clocks don't stop for a broken man's heart.
Life is still out there, no matter how far away I run.

The Pain Of Getting Pricked By A Thorn

He asked me to trust him.
To ignore his devilish grin.
To forget the way his eyes sparkled each time he wounded my heart.
He asked me to trust him.
To love a rose tangled in its thorns.

Puzzle Pieces

He found her as one.
Broke her into pieces.
And when all the damage was done,
he left her for someone else to put back together.

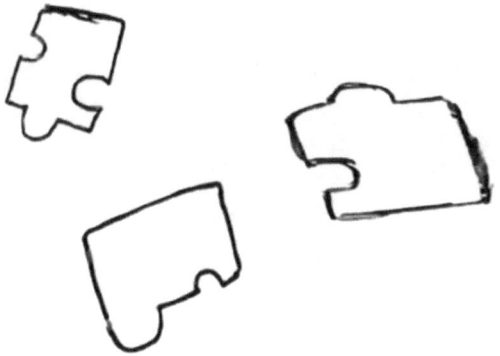

Disgrace To Society

You used me, and once you were done,
I was thrown away like a dirty napkin.
And as I laid in the trash among thousands of pieces of filth,
I began to immerse myself until I, too, was nothing but filth.
People walked by.
Looks of disgust smeared across their faces.
They turned their heads and ignored my presence.
I must've offended them.
The scars against my fragile skin, no one wants to see.
The pain in my choked-up voice, no one wants to hear.

The Girl You Never Noticed

Her eyes are glued open, never blinking.
Watching as the world passes her by.
Colors, people, and animals reflect off the glassy windows to her soul.
Oblivious to the life that continues to exist around her.
Seeing but never processing.
Her thoughts have vanished like ghosts.
Fleeing somewhere else.
Somewhere better, where they can be free, flying among the birds.
Still, the poor girl remains motionless.
Her body has given up.
Quiet is the poor girl who lives in the utter silence of her mind.

Mother

Although you cry, you are not broken.
You whisper how you wish to surrender.
I crave nothing more than to take the pain within your innocent eyes away.
I'd feel it for you, so you don't have to.
Your tears bleed against my shoulder as I hold you in my arms.
I squeeze you tight,
bringing you in closer.
Maybe if I hold you long enough, the love I carry will seep its way into your heart.

Soap And Water

The words you whispered long ago still haunt me.
Like glue, they're attached to my skin.
Eating me alive as I frantically try to wash them off.

Death At My Doorstep

Nothing I say could describe what it's like
watching someone leave you
when you can't do anything to stop them.

Don't Forget Me

When I see you next, caterpillars will be butterflies.
When I see you next, flowers will bloom.
When I see you next, the world's heavy weight will disappear.

But if I'm too late…

I'll stumble across an open terrain with no trace of life.
I'll see gray clouds hovering above my head as it pours.
And at that moment, the world's strength will crush me into hundreds of small pieces.
Too small for you to notice.
Too small, you'll think I never came.

Song Of Your Heart

Every night you hold me in my dreams.
You hold me tight in the clear silence of the night.
And at this moment, I'm at peace.
Your arms wrapped around me, pulling me close.
You are my home, and the beating of your heart is the song I treasure.

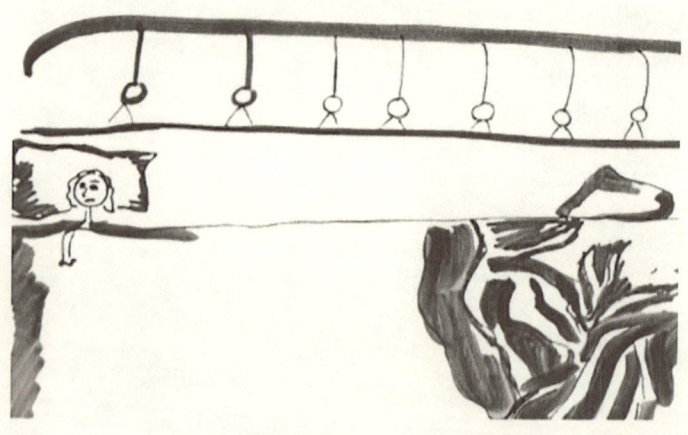

Song Of Your Heart

There came one night when you held tight.
The night was still silent, but the sky was no longer clear.
This was the moment I had feared.
Your arms wrapped around me.
And yet, I sense you hesitate before pulling me closer.
Though you do, I wish you had not.
For now, you're no longer my haven, and the song your heart used to sing has ended.

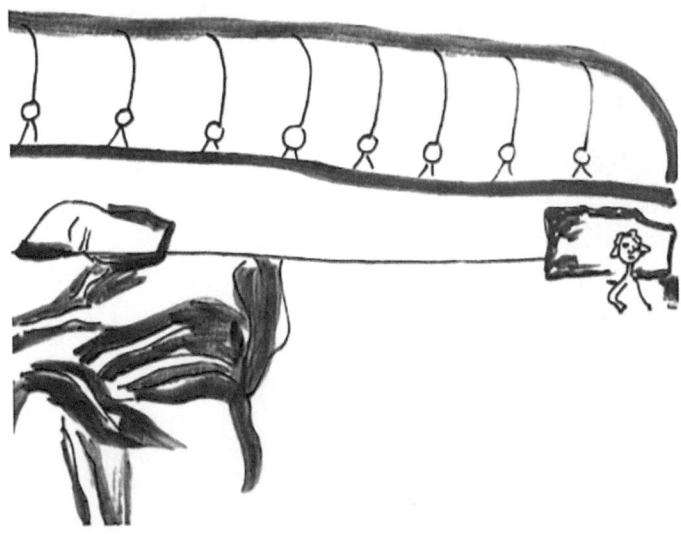

Wounded Heart

How can I protect myself
when I've run out of bricks to build the walls with?

Burning Out

Within my stomach, a vicious torch has been lit.
Its blaze spreads as I study myself in the mirror.
Like a switch, I turn off the painful thoughts that race inside my head.
I take in what stares back,
but the mere sight of my reflection is enough for the switch to turn back on.
The thoughts grow louder as they become voices that wrap around the body I hate.
The fire rages.
Its hot sparks sting my skin.
"Get me out," I wail, except no one is around.
No one hears me cry.

Life Without You

In another universe,
there is a version of me that never met you.
How I envy their life.

Even Mother Nature Cries

I went on a walk today.
It poured, but that's okay.
I like walking in the rain.
It hides the tears that stream from my eyes.

Too Late

It was clear.
When the sun set for the last time.
When the bird sang before it died.
When he said his last goodbye,
she was in love.

What's Going On Next Door

The house felt bigger once you left.
Maybe because now my feet drag against the wooden floor
with every step I take.
But I'd like to think it's because I rearranged the
furniture, trying to erase the memory of who used to live here.
Two souls full of hope and ambition.
If only we had known how lost we truly were.
Perhaps you would have never moved in.

After You Left

Time went out the door and took her love with it.
Tears rolled down the child's tired face.
"Why are you sad, little girl?
The pain is over.
The war has been fought, and you won."
But her tears weren't of one in mourning.
Rather a hostage finally free.

One of the most powerful human traits is the ability to provide one's own sense of closure.

Flower Child

Build yourself up as if you're planting a flower.
You start with the seeds in your hands.
So tiny, so fragile.
"How could anything possibly come from these little specks?"
you will ask yourself.
But stay around.
Do not lose hope.
For one day, you will be a sunflower, standing tall and strong against the wind.

Soon You Will Be Free

What they don't tell you about recovery
is it's easier to get there than to
stay there. Somedays will feel harder than others.
The minutes will turn into hours; during this time,
you may question whether you're strong enough.
You are. You can climb mountains. You
can swim the length of oceans.
You can get better because you are
you, and *you* are all you need.

Among The Stars

There lived a boy who loved to dance the night away
in his peaceful garden under the glistening stars.
It was silent when he danced.
No one around to see.
He did this until the hairs on his head turned grey.
When his legs could barely hold him up, the old man stopped.
Spending his nights watching the stars from his window,
longing to dance under their light once more.
One night, the stars were shining brighter than usual.
With all his strength, he carried himself back into the garden.
As he danced, the stars sang a beautiful hymn.
Tears fell against his wrinkled skin.
The stars had watched him grow up, and now they called to him,
building the man a staircase for him to climb.
Lost in their beauty, he may have been.
But home, he finally was.

Beneath The Snow

A winter's storm.
I'm not sure why it comforts me.
Maybe it's the howling of the wind, hoping to be heard.
Or perhaps it's the endless snowflakes
that blanket the ground,
hiding what remains below the surface.

Know Your Worth

You stopped looking in the mirror, fearing what would be looking back.
They had a sick view of the world and tried to make you believe it.

You are so much stronger than you know.

Now they're gone, and you're left with nothing but the pieces of a girl.
But before you can make yourself whole, you must learn to heal.
Learn to love again.
Learn to laugh again.
Reclaim your worth again.

Reclaim your world

Again.

State Of Mind

Just because you can't always see the sun
doesn't mean it's not always there.

Strength In Kindness

To fill our words with hate and our minds
with harm is an easy thing to do.
To acknowledge the urge and still not give in
is what I hope for you.

The Places We Could Go

Let's go on an adventure.
Let's leave our worries behind as our feet carry us further.
Freedom will ring, and we'll sing along.
Hearts full of excitement.
Minds at peace.
Maybe we'll end up at a beach.
Calm waves splash against our toes, and the sun smiles at us.
Maybe we'll end up in a field of flowers.
Lovely colors bring out your eyes, and the aromas feed
our hearts.
Maybe we'll end up in a lively city.
Mesmerized by the bright lights above our heads
and the busy town that keeps us awake.
When you're with me, there's no telling the places we can go.

Imaginary Friends

There was a time when my imagination soared.
If flew so high it created life in empty rooms
and I formed friends that were always by my side.
Who comforted me when I scraped my knee.
Held me when I couldn't sleep.
But as time passed, I grew too old for these silly games.
I abandoned them.
Erased them from my mind.
But my biggest regret is forgetting to say goodbye.
I wonder where imaginary friends go to die.

Joyous Life

Joy is flowers beginning to bud at the end of a storm.
It's the feeling of reconnecting with someone you thought you'd lost.
Joy is more than a smile.
More than a laugh.
Joy is what motivates us.
Even in our darkest times and most vulnerable moments, joy is still with us.
Sometimes people mistake the intensity of sadness for the absence of joy.
But this is not the case.
For joy is all around us.
It's embedded in the earth's floor.
It's in the sky above our heads.
It can be found in all our victories, big and small.
Waking up each morning is a victory, don't you think?
Our bodies awakening to the endless possibilities of a new day is a victory, don't you see?
You being here with me is a victory,
I so believe.

Another Woman's Beauty

Edgar Allen Poe once said, "Another
woman's beauty is not the
absence of your own." When I first
read these words, I felt a
shift within me. A light bulb had
gone off. An epiphany had
taken place. I saw the world differently.
I saw others differently.
I saw myself differently. Like a snake shedding its skin,
everything had changed. Like a
newborn baby, a fresh start had
begun. Oh, how I wish I could've read
those words sooner. How
I wish I could build a time machine
and tell myself these exact
words five years ago. I would've gone
about my day repeating
them like a mantra until I believed
them. Until I internalized it.
I'd let these words form a sanctuary
around my body, bringing
peace to my heart and mind.
Leaving their mark in the
footprints of each step I take, hoping
whoever walks behind me
embraces these wise words as well.

The One

I like to think of breakups as
being one step closer
to finding your soulmate.

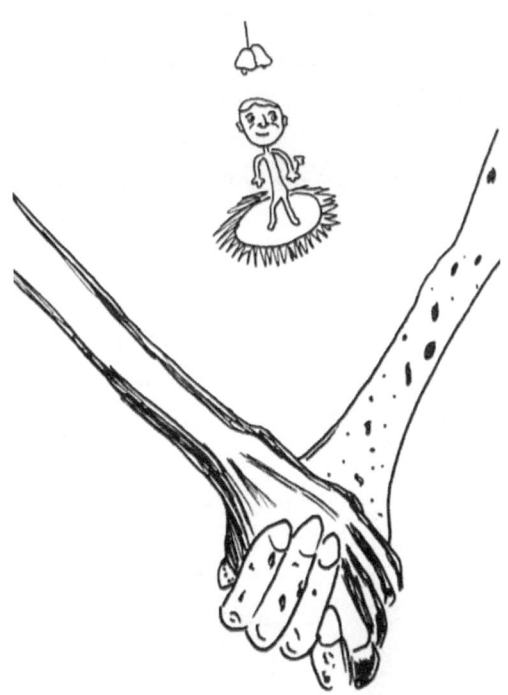

Fuel For The Spirit

There comes a time late at night
when the wind blows, and I
have no choice but to follow.
It desperately calls for me, longing for my presence.
Maybe it's the mysterious night sky
that holds the glistening
light of the stars that makes me feel so pure.
Or possibly it's the rare silence of the world around me.
Regardless, at this moment, my soul
is fed, my heart is filled.
I am reborn.
For it's just me and mother nature awake.
As for you, you're kept hidden under blankets of safety.
You foolishly sleep through the climax.
You ignore the beautiful night and its enchantment.
An opportunity was blown over your head.
Do you realize your mistake and open your eyes?
That I do not know because, like the
wind that once called me,
I've already left to explore the wonders of our world.
And as I embark on this journey, adventure fuels my spirit.
It lifts me into that dark sky I once told you about.
It grasps me, holds me, and I become one with nature.
I cannot escape.
Should I panic?
No, this is my calling.
My purpose.

Lifted above the world, I can only wish
you, too, have opened your
eyes to the calling of the wind.
And if you do, I pray you will embark
on your own journey
Where you'll find me here painting the sky.

Growing Up In A Forest

I'm from a place where trees are skyscrapers.
Where my neighbor is a family of deer.
I'm from a place where the color green runs freely.
Where foxes are lurking and bunnies are playing.
I'm from a place where the flow of water can always be heard.
Where flowers grow in every direction.
I'm from a place of beauty.
Of nature.
I'm from a place that becomes more scarce with each day that goes by.
Each tree slashed.
Each animal pierced.
I'm from a place where people come to be rejuvenated
by our innocence.
The innocence they once had.

Anticipation

I feel a sudden rush of nervousness glide over me.
Wanting to retreat.
Urging to turn back.
I must ground myself.
No matter how shaky my hands may get or how antsy my legs may feel.
I must control these flying creatures within my stomach.
They're not there to tell me to leave.
They're here to help me stay.
That this is important.
That this is just a new door presenting itself.
And although I may not know what's on the other side,
I am human.
And humans are destined to explore.

Perspective

The idea nothing lasts forever may scare you.
It may twist your stomach into millions of knots.
Pull your body in different directions.
It may leave you feeling helpless.
Keep you up at night.

Or it may calm you.
Knowing even the disturbing thoughts your innocent mind carries are not forever.
It may remind you of your strength.
That you can remain grounded in times of chaos.
It may show you how beautiful you are.
As you realize, the only thing that defines you is yourself.

Life Worth Living

"The unexamined life is not worth living" *Socrates*.
So I ask, when do humans learn most about themselves?
It's when we're stripped of our pride like a flower cut
from its stem.
It's when we're exposed like a deer in the headlights.
It's when we hurt, like a child skinning its knee against the
playground.
For its pain, discomfort and shame that you will
grow from.
You must first fall to be given the
opportunity to get back up.

Deforestation

Wrapped within my broken bones,
you rest in my arms.
Unfazed by the icy frost that coats my skin.
But somewhere, buried within the deep, snowy storm
of my heart,
you've created warmth.
And there, you manage to fall asleep.

Hummingbird

Does the hummingbird still sing?
Why has it been so long since I last heard its
precious voice?
You may find it humorous it's still on my mind.
That the songs of the hummingbird still ring in my ears.
But I am hopeful and patient.
If you need me, I will be by my window where the
hummingbird used to rest.
Though if you arrive, hold your tongue.
Join me as I try listening to the hummingbird's next melody.

Love's Touch

I want to feel love again.
Oh, how I long for love's touch.
How I miss its warmth against my skin.

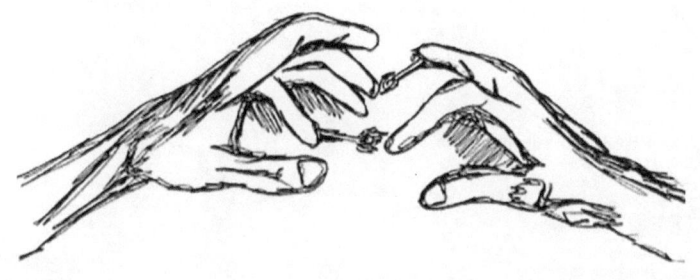

The Point Of Life

And the child asked,
"Sing me a song of hope, of life, of happiness.
Sing me a song that makes life worth living."
But the old man's lips stayed closed.
He told the child,
"You are responsible for creating your own song."

FIN.

And yet, here you are, having survived it all.

www.ingramcontent.com/pod-product-compliance
Lightning Source LLC
Chambersburg PA
CBHW030536080526
44585CB00014B/963